D1274391

FIRST BIOGRAPHIES

Kit Carson

Published by Raintree Steck-Vaughn Publishers, an imprint of Steck-Vaughn Company

Retold for young readers by Edith Vann
Editor: Pam Wells
Project Manager: Julie Klaus
Electronic Production: Scott Melcer

Library of Congress Cataloging-in-Publication Data

Gleiter, Jan, 1947-
Kit Carson / Jan Gleiter and Kathleen Thompson; illustrated by Rick Whipple
p. cm. — (First biographies)
ISBN 0-8114-8455-6 hardcover library binding
ISBN 0-8114-9352-0 softcover binding
1. Carson, Kit, 1809-1868 — Juvenile literature. 2. Pioneers — West (U.S.) — Biography — Juvenile literature. 3. Scouts and scouting — West (U.S.) — Biography — Juvenile literature. 4. Soldiers — West (U.S.) — Biography — Juvenile literature. 5. West (U.S.) — Biography — Juvenile literature. [1. Carson, Kit, 1809-1868 . 2. Pioneers. 3. West (U.S.) — Biography.] I. Gleiter, Jan, 1947-. II. Thompson, Kathleen. III. Whipple, Rick. IV. Title. V. Series.
F592.C53G54 1995
978'.02'092 — dc20 94-41000
[B] CIP AC

Printed and bound in China
7 8 9 10 11 WKT 07 06 05 04 03

FIRST BIOGRAPHIES

Kit Carson

Jan Gleiter and Kathleen Thompson
Illustrated by Rick Whipple

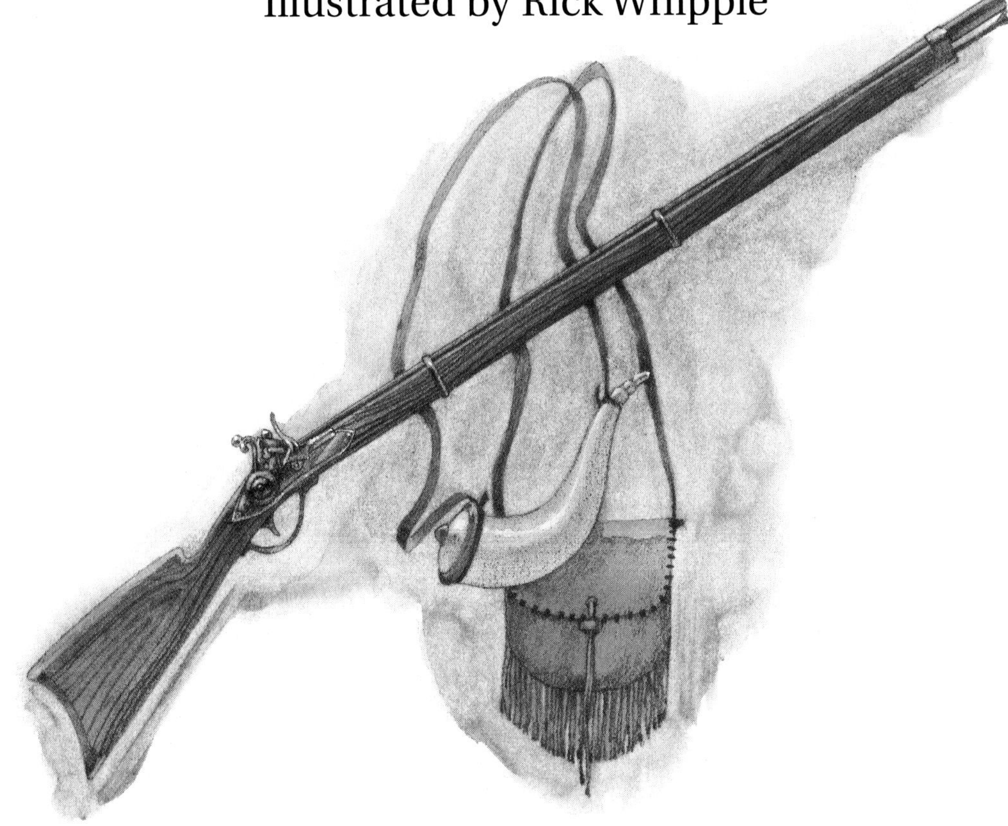

RAINTREE STECK-VAUGHN PUBLISHERS
The Steck-Vaughn Company

Austin, Texas

The Carsons and the Boones never stayed in one place for long. They did not want to settle down. Instead they wanted to see new places. First they moved from Scotland to America. Then from Pennsylvania to Kentucky. Later they moved from Kentucky to Missouri. They seemed happiest finding out about places they had never seen.

In 1811 the Carsons moved to Missouri. Young Kit was not even two. It was a long, hard trip. Now the Carsons had found a brand new place.

When Kit was older, he hunted and fished with Daniel Boone. By that time Daniel was an old man. But he was still a great hunter. He showed young Kit how to track animals and shoot them. Kit learned from Daniel to respect the ways of Native Americans.

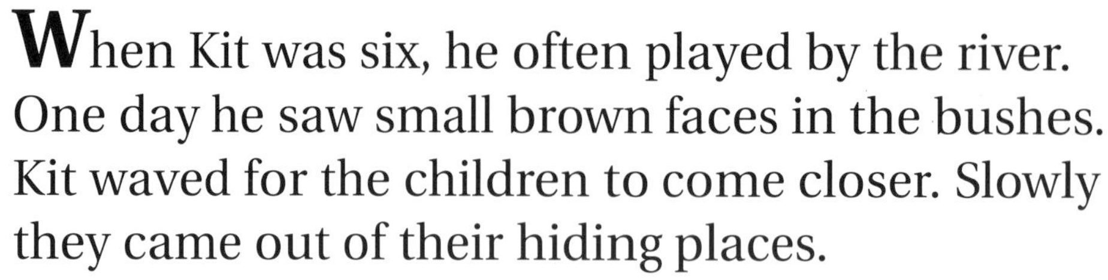

When Kit was six, he often played by the river. One day he saw small brown faces in the bushes. Kit waved for the children to come closer. Slowly they came out of their hiding places.

Kit pointed to himself and said his name. No answer. He did it again. Then he pointed at a Native American boy. The boy said his name.

Soon Kit knew all the children's names. They showed him how to play a game with sticks. Then he showed them how to play a game. They didn't use the same words for things. But it didn't matter. They understood each other anyway.

When Kit was fifteen, he went to work. He helped a man named Workman, who made saddles. Kit was to stay a year. Workman taught him to make saddles. But Kit was very unhappy there.

Kit missed the forest and the river. He dreamed of the West. He wanted to hunt buffalo. Most of all he wanted to see wild places.

Kit heard about some men who buy and sell things. These traders were going west, to Santa Fe. His older brothers wouldn't let him go. They thought he was too young.

Well, Kit thought he was old enough. He borrowed a mule. Then he left for Independence, Missouri, a hundred miles away.

Kit asked the traders to take him west with them. He was not very big. The traders just laughed at him. Still Kit did not give up. One of the leaders thought Kit was brave. He said that Kit could come along. He could take care of the animals. So Kit started out for New Mexico.

By November they were in Santa Fe. There were sixty wagons and one hundred men. Everyone came out to see the big wagon train.

Kit went with a small group of traders from Santa Fe to Taos. There he met his father's old friend Kincaid. Kincaid was a trapper and an explorer.

That winter Kit stayed with Kincaid in the New Mexico hills. Kit learned Spanish from him. He learned some Native American languages and their sign language. Kit also learned the ways of native peoples of the Southwest.

Kincaid made maps on the ground with a stick. They showed places few people had ever seen. Kincaid helped Kit learn all that he could.

Kit made things to wear out of furs and animal skins. The two men made beds out of corn husks. They covered them with buffalo robes.

Kit learned to cook. He also learned how to dry meat. It had to last a long time without going bad. Kit made friends with the Native Americans who lived near Taos.

When Kit was twenty, he met Ewing Young. He had heard about Kit. Also he wanted Kit to hunt with his party. Kit said he would go along.

For the next twelve years, Kit hunted and trapped animals. He worked for the Rocky Mountain Fur Company. He lived and worked with mountain men. Still Taos was his home. Kit always went back there.

Kit knew Native American ways and often kept other trappers out of trouble. He was able to talk to both sides. Many times he settled their fights. Sometimes there was fighting anyway. Right or wrong, Kit would always fight for his friends, the trappers.

On one trip the men camped near some Arapaho. Kit was twenty-five. He met a beautiful young Arapaho woman named Waa-nibe.

Kit fell in love with her, and they were married. Two years later they had a daughter named Adaline.

When Adaline was very young, her mother died. Kit took her to his family in Missouri. His family made the pretty little girl feel at home. Then she started going to the Rock Springs School.

Kit stayed for a while. Then he had to go to St. Louis. On the way home Kit met a man who would change his life.

Kit Carson and Lieutenant John Charles Frémont met on a steamboat. They talked about the West. Frémont's job was to explore the land between Missouri and the Rocky Mountains. He was looking for men to go with him, and he needed a guide.

Kit told Frémont he could take him any place he wanted to go. Frémont gave Kit the job.

Kit Carson was a guide for Charles Frémont on three trips. He carried letters from Frémont to government people in Washington, D.C. Then he carried letters back. These trips helped Americans find out about the West. They also made Kit Carson famous for his courage and his skill.

Kit Carson became a messenger between the government and the Ute. For most of his life, Kit had fought on the side of the settlers. But he had lived with the Ute and learned their ways. The Ute had been his friends for a long time. Now he could speak for them.

Kit had strong beliefs. Many who should have protected the Native Americans lied to them. People would fight them and take their land. Kit said much of the fighting was not the Indians' fault.

Years later people talked about Kit Carson. They told how he could track anything on two feet or four. People remembered that Kit was a good man. He wanted the best for all Americans.

Key Dates

1809	Born in Madison County, Kentucky.
1811	Moved with his family to the Missouri frontier.
1824	Was sent to work for a saddlemaker. Kit did not like this indoor work.
1826	Ran away with a group of traders. He went to Santa Fe and Taos in what is now New Mexico.
1829-1841	Was guide, hunter, and trapper for different groups of explorers and traders.
1842-1845	Was guide for John C. Frémont, who explored the West. Kit Carson became famous for his skills and courage.
1846	Fought in the Mexican War.
1853	Became U.S. agent for the Ute.
1861-1865	Fought for the Union in the Civil War.
1865	He became a brigadier general.
1868	Went to Washington with a group of Ute to help them. He became sick and went home to Colorado. He died on May 23.